LIVING
NO SHAME
OUT
NO CHAINS
LOUD

DRAY ORION

For the ones who lit the match in me,

the ones who never tried to put it out,

and for every soul still dragging chains—

may you set the world on fire.

If you counted me out—then you miscounted.

~DRAY ORION

CONTENTS

Introduction ix

PART ONE
SETTING THE FIRE

1. The Firestarter — 3
2. Gas to the Flame — 7
3. Born Chained — 11
4. The Lie of the Cage — 15
5. Living Unchained — 19

PART TWO
LIVING UNCHAINED

6. Burn Without Apology — 23
7. When the Fire Flickers — 27
8. What Freedom Feels Like — 31
9. The Cost of Staying Small — 35
10. The First Step Hurts Like Hell — 39

PART THREE
BECOMING THE FIRE

11. Living on Fire — 45
12. The Silence After — 49
13. Born of Fire — 51
14. The Firekeeper — 55
15. The Way You Burn — 59
16. Living Out Loud — 63

Epilogue — 67

INTRODUCTION

This is not a self-help book.
Not a motivational poster in chapter form.
No hollow affirmations, no sugar, no lies.

This is a manifesto.
A reckoning.
A fire in your chest you've been trying to smother for too long.

I didn't write this to save you,
but because I couldn't keep carrying it alone.

Because I've been chained.
By shame.
By silence.
By expectations I never agreed to.
By roles I was forced to play just to survive the damn day.

I broke those chains one by one—
Some with rage, some with heartbreak,
and some with a quiet kind of courage I didn't know I had.

INTRODUCTION

And every link that fell became a word.
Every scar, a sentence.
Every moment I almost gave up, a page.

That's how this was born.

This isn't about perfection.
It's about truth.
It's about fire.
About choosing to stop shrinking, hiding,
and editing yourself for people who never saw you clearly in the first place.

This book does not hold your hand.
It's a book that hands you a match.

I can't promise comfort.
I can promise this:

If you've ever
felt like the world was too heavy for the version of you they never let live—
looked in the mirror and seen more flame than flesh—
felt the weight of chains you were told you needed—

This is for you.

This is your permission.
This is your dare.
This is your reflection staring back and shouting:
No shame. No chains. Not anymore.

So read it how you need to.
Sit with it. Fight with it. Throw it across the room if you have to.
But when you come back—

INTRODUCTION

bring your fire.

Because you don't have to stay quiet.
You don't have to stay small, subdued, and smoldering.
And you damn sure don't have to stay chained.

PART ONE
SETTING THE FIRE

ONE
THE FIRESTARTER

I was born into a world that told me who I was, before I ever had the chance to decide.
They handed me chains before I even knew I had a choice.
They called them rules. Called them expectations. Called them tradition.
Called them love.
But I know the weight of a cage when I feel one.

They taught me to sit still, stay quiet, and take what I was given.
To carry the weight with a smile and call it strength.
To swallow the fire and call it discipline.
To hide the scars and call it survival.

I call it bullshit.

They wanted me to be a lesson.
A warning.
A man who'd learned to kneel.
But I don't kneel.
I don't ask permission to exist.
And I sure as hell don't apologize for the fire in my blood.

Because every time they tried to break me, they only fed the flame.
Every rule, every lie, every expectation—

gasoline.

So now?
Now, I burn.

I burn for the nights spent drowning in my thoughts.
For the ghosts that walk beside me, whispering of wars long ended.
For the scars I wear like armor.
And the battles I didn't ask for, but fought anyway.

I burn for the times I was told to be ashamed—for being too much, too loud, too different, too wrong—and for every moment I was asked to make myself smaller to fit into their world.

I will not shrink.
I will not soften.
I will not break to make you more comfortable.

If my truth offends you, look away.
If my fire is too bright, step back.
If my existence makes your hands shake—good.
Let them tremble.

I spent years doing time—locked in the past, bound by expectations, drowning in guilt that was never mine to carry.
Not anymore.
Not ever again.

I am fire. I am freedom.
And I will not wear chains that were never mine.

So, I say this to you—to the ones still afraid to burn, the ones still holding onto the chains they were given:
Let them go.
Drop them.
Watch them turn to ash in the heat of your fire.

LIVING OUT LOUD

No more shame.
No more chains.
No more waiting for the world to tell you it's okay to be who you are.

Burn.

TWO
GAS TO THE FLAME

Fire like mine doesn't just erupt out of nowhere.
It's built—spark by spark, scar by scar.
And every time the world tried to smother me, they only gave me more to burn.

The world never ran out of gas to throw on me.

It didn't matter how small the spark was. Or if I tried to burn quietly, tucked into corners where no one could see me. Somehow, the gas would find me—heavy, thick, and stinking of opportunity disguised as ruin—and every time, the fire inside me would flare, wild and unpredictable, leaping higher than before.

There were days I thought about snuffing myself out completely. Days when the cost of burning felt heavier than the reward.
You can't burn constantly without paying for it with your own skin.
You can't light the way without being the first one scorched.
I learned that truth young, but it took years to accept it without apology.

They told me to stay small.
They told me to burn politely.
But polite flames can't survive storms.

Polite flames don't change the temperature of a room just by walking into it.

So I stayed loud. I stayed hot.
I blazed through every label, every limit, every expectation they tried to smother me with.
They never smothered me—they could only feed me.
Every ounce of doubt, every insult, every whispered judgment—fuel.
Gas to the flame.

At first, I thought the fire was something that needed to be managed. Controlled.
Tamed, so I could fit better in the neat little lives everyone else seemed so proud of.

I tried that once.
I built a life out of other people's blueprints—thinking maybe they knew something I didn't—
and it was the coldest I'd ever felt.

You can build yourself a house out of fear, out of good intentions, out of silence.
But a house like that isn't a home—it's a prison.
I didn't last long before the fire tore through the walls and sent me running, heart pounding, soul raw and gasping for air.

I'm not here to be contained.
I'm here to ignite everything I touch.
Not for destruction—for illumination. For truth. For life.

The world will keep throwing gas. That's a promise.
People love the idea of a fire until they realize it's not just for their warmth—it's for burning down the bullshit, too.

Let them come.

LIVING OUT LOUD

Let them pour it on.
All they're doing is giving me more to burn.

THREE
BORN CHAINED

I was born into a world with chains ready and waiting the minute I opened my eyes.

They said it was for my safety.
For my future.
For my soul.

But it was really about control.
It was always about control.

They handed me labels before I knew what they meant.
Boy.
Man.
Son.
Soldier.
Provider.

Titles stacked like *shackles* around my neck before I ever chose a damn thing.

But at first?
I wore them proudly.
I thought that's what life was supposed to feel like—
Heavy.

Restrained.
Tolerated.
Muted.

But pride festers into resentment when you realize you were never meant to be free.
You were just meant to perform.

Smile the right smile.
Say the right words.
Live the right life.

If the chains cut too deep—crushing your chest until you forgot how to breathe—that was just the cost of being "good."

But here's the truth they didn't teach:
You are not broken for wanting more.
You are not ungrateful for feeling the weight.
You are not wrong for dreaming about fire when all they offer you are cages.

You were never born to be chained.

You were born to *burn*.

And no matter how long you've been bound, the key has always been the same:
You.

Your fire.
Your refusal.
Your first furious, trembling, unapologetic step toward yourself.

No one is coming to save you.
You have to burn your own way out.

And once you do?

There's no going back.

FOUR
THE LIE OF THE CAGE

But the cage is comfortable.

At first, you think it's hell.
A prison.
You rage against it.
You hate it.
You swear you'll never settle.

Then you stay.

Why?
Because they built it just for you.

It fits.
It holds.
It keeps you in place.

And after a while?

You stop noticing the bars.

You decorate the walls.
You find routines that make it bearable.
You tell yourself it's not that bad.

You call it home.

Because stepping out?
That's unknown.
That's risk.
That world out there doesn't come with a script.

So, you settle.

You keep your voice down.
You keep your head down.
You keep your fire down.

And that's exactly what they want.

Because they don't have to chain you to keep you here,
just make you afraid of leaving.

They don't need whips or walls,
just your fear of what happens without them.

That's how they keep you small.

But let me tell you something:
That cage was never for your protection.
It was for theirs.

Because they saw what you could be.
They knew what you would become.
And it scared the *hell* out of them.

So, they built a cage and blinded you with a story—
"This is where you belong."
"This is all you're meant to be."

And you believed it.

Until now.

Because here's the truth:
The cage doesn't lock from the outside.
It never did.

And the second you stop believing in it?
It falls apart.

So the question isn't can you leave?
It's will you?

Will you tear down what was built to contain you?
Step into the fire you were told to fear?
Burn for something greater than their comfort?

Because if you're waiting for permission…
You'll rot.
You'll disappear.
You'll burn out.
You'll die.
All in that cage.

FIVE
LIVING UNCHAINED

Freedom isn't comfortable.
It's raw.
It's terrifying.
It's waking up every day with no map, no guarantees—and stepping into the unknown anyway.

Living unchained isn't weightless.
It means owning the weight of your choices rather than your chains.
It means letting go of the neat little cages that once kept you predictable, acceptable, safe.

It means not everyone will clap for you.
Some will fear you.
Some will leave you.

Let them.

You weren't meant to carry the world's comfort on your back.
You were meant to carry your own fire forward.

Living unchained isn't about never feeling fear—
It's about refusing to let fear chain you to a life you've already outgrown.
I'm not saying don't be afraid.

I'm saying don't let fear make your decisions for you.

It's about trusting that the rawness you feel is a sign you're alive.
It's about remembering that breaking free isn't a one-time event.
It's a choice you make, over and over again.

Some days, you'll sprint toward your future.
Other days, you'll crawl.
Every day you refuse to rebuild the cage—

You win.

You don't owe the world your silence.
You don't owe them your smaller, easier, quieter self.

You owe them your truth.
You owe them your fire.
And you owe yourself the life you were born to live—
Not the life you were tricked into accepting.

Living unchained is messy.
It's fierce.
It's lonely sometimes.

But it's real.
And it's yours.

And that's enough.

PART TWO
LIVING UNCHAINED

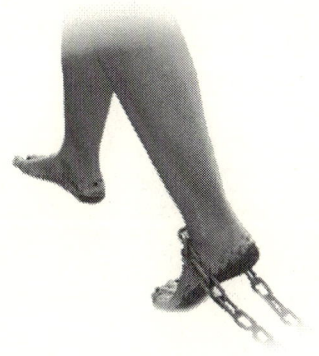

SIX
BURN WITHOUT APOLOGY

You don't owe anyone an explanation for your fire.
You don't owe anyone your softness, silence, or surrender.

You weren't made to be palatable.
You weren't made to fit into the tidy little boxes they hand out to people who dream too small to be dangerous.

You were made to burn.

Burn through the lies you were taught to believe.
Burn through the masks they forced you to wear.
Burn through the guilt they draped over your shoulders like a burial shroud.

You are not too much.
You are exactly enough.

They will call you reckless.
They will call you selfish.
They will call you cruel.

Let them.

They do not know the cost of staying small.
They have never carried a fire like yours and lived to tell about it.

You don't have to make yourself digestible.
You don't have to twist yourself into shapes that make people more comfortable.

You were not born to be understood by those who fear the flame.

You were born to *burn without apology*.

And once you do?
There's nothing they can build that will ever cage you again.

Though they will try.
They'll throw every fear they have at you, dressed up with pretty names like "responsibility" and "maturity" and "common sense."

They'll tell you that burning too brightly is dangerous… that flying too high is selfish… that standing too tall is arrogant.

But listen carefully:
That's not love talking.
That's fear.

And it's not your job to carry their fear for them.

You were never meant to fold yourself down to fit inside their comfort zones.
You were never meant to trade your fire for their approval.

They can call you anything they want.

Wild.
Reckless.

LIVING OUT LOUD

Uncontrollable.

Take it as a compliment.

Because wild things aren't meant to be caged.
Reckless things aren't afraid to live.
Uncontrollable things don't ask for permission.

You are not an apology.
You are not a mistake.
You are not something that needs to be hidden away to make the world feel safer.

You are a force.

And the second you decide to burn without apology—
the second you stop trying to explain your fire, excuse it, tame it—
the world has two choices:

1) Rise to meet you
2) Get the hell out of your way

So burn.

Louder.
Hotter.
Fiercer.

Not because they said you could.
Not because they finally decided you were worthy.

But because you were worthy from the first breath you ever took.

And no one—not them, not their fears, not their cages—gets to put that fire out.

Not anymore.

Not ever again.

SEVEN
WHEN THE FIRE FLICKERS

They don't tell you this part.

That even the brightest fire can falter.
That even the ones who refuse to kneel will, sometimes, fall to one knee just to catch their breath.
That burning doesn't always mean *roaring*—sometimes it's *surviving*.
Smoldering. Gritting your teeth and daring the darkness to try.

There are nights when the fire flickers.
When it dwindles so far you wonder if it's even still there.
When the silence is louder than your heartbeat, and the weight of everything you've carried tries to crush your ribs from the inside out.

You start thinking, *maybe the cage would be easier.*
Maybe the chains were lighter than the battles I'm fighting now.
Maybe shrinking back wouldn't hurt as much as standing tall with broken bones.

That's the lie whispering to you.

Because the world wants you tired.
Wants you doubting.
Wants you crawling back—bloodied hands, cracked spirit—begging

for a smaller, quieter version of yourself that fits inside their fragile idea of normal.

But not you.

Not now.

Because inside you—even on weary nights when the fire flickers—there's a truth they can't kill:

You don't owe this world your surrender.

You don't owe it your silence, your smallness, your broken spirit wrapped in pretty apologies.

You owe it your roar.

You owe it your flame.

And even if all you have left is one trembling ember, deep in your chest—
that's enough.

Because fire doesn't die in the dark.
It waits.
It learns.
It gathers itself in the stillness,
and—when the moment comes—it erupts.

So let them think you're finished.
Let them see you stumble, see you gasp for air, see you fall silent.
Let them believe the flicker means you're fading.

Then show them what happens when a soul like yours catches again.

LIVING OUT LOUD

Show them that fire never asks permission to rise.

EIGHT
WHAT FREEDOM FEELS LIKE

Freedom doesn't whisper.
It roars.

It's not some soft, tender thing you cradle in your hands as if it might break.
It's brutal. It's wild.
It surges, like cold air in burned lungs—painful, shocking, undeniable.

Freedom is the scream you swallowed years ago finally tearing out of your throat.
It's the sound of your own footsteps walking away from everything that tried to own you.

It's not neat.
It's not polite.
It's raw, loud, and tastes like blood and salt and sky.

You don't ask if you deserve it.
You seize it.

Because after everything you survived—after every scar, every betrayal, every lonely night spent doubting yourself—
you earned this.

And no one gets to take it back.

Freedom doesn't feel safe at first.
It feels like falling.
It feels like standing on a cliff's edge with the whole world screaming at you to step back—
and choosing to jump instead.

It feels like betrayal to the ones who built your cage.
It feels like selfishness to the ones who only loved you when you stayed small.

Good.
Let it.

Because this life—this fire-breathing, raw-knuckled, blood-and-bone life—
was never meant to be measured by how many people you kept comfortable.

It's meant to be measured by how alive you let yourself become.

Freedom tastes like breath you thought you lost.
It sounds like your own voice, unfiltered, unapologetic, unbreakable.

It feels like standing in the wreckage of everything that tried to kill you
—and smiling defiantly because they failed.

It feels like not needing permission anymore.
Not asking for a seat.
Not begging for a voice.
Taking your place—because it was always yours.

There will be days you stumble.
Days the old chains will whisper promises in the dark—
"It was easier inside."

LIVING OUT LOUD

"It was safer when you were small."

Lies.

You weren't made for cages.
You weren't built to be easy, or small, or silent.

You weren't just born for the storm.
You are the storm.
And freedom—true freedom—feels like remembering that,
every single time the world tries to make you forget.

NINE
THE COST OF STAYING SMALL

They don't warn you about the real cost.
Not when they hand you the chains.
Not when they tell you to be grateful.
Not when they teach you how to disappear in plain sight.

They tell you small is safe.
Small is smart.
Small is survival.

But they don't tell you what it steals.

How staying small hollows you out from the inside.
How every dream you bury corrodes into bitterness.
How every truth you swallow poisons your blood a little more.
How the cage doesn't just hold your body—it dims your soul.
How hope sours the longer you keep it caged.

Staying small costs you your fire.
Your voice.
Your wildness.
Your goddamn self.

It costs you the nights you could've danced beneath stars you were too afraid to chase.

It costs you the love you could've built if you hadn't been so busy apologizing for existing.
It costs you the version of you that was never meant to be polite, or easy, or palatable.

And worst of all?
It costs you time.

Years spent living a life that doesn't fit.
Seasons spent waiting for permission that was never going to come.
Moments you can't get back.

That's the real cruelty of the cage.

Not the walls.
Not the rules.
Not even the chains.

It's the time it steals from you, all the while you convince yourself you're better off inside it.

Let me be clear:

There is no prize for staying small.
There is no trophy for out-shrinking your pain.
There is no medal for making yourself invisible.

There's just regret.
And a slow death, measured in what-ifs and almosts.

You were never meant to be small.
You were never meant to fold yourself into corners and beg for scraps of space.

You were born to take up room.
To burn loud.

To breathe fire.

And every second you stay small is a second you betray the wild, beautiful thing you were meant to become.

So if you're standing at the edge—
feeling the pull toward something bigger, something raw and terrifying and real—
don't you dare look away.

Don't you dare stay small because it's what they expect.

They will mourn the comfortable version of you.
Let them.

You?

You've got a fire to set—for every version of you they tried to smother.

TEN
THE FIRST STEP HURTS LIKE HELL

Nobody tells you this part, either.

They talk about freedom like it's some beautiful sunrise you just walk into, arms wide open, finally at peace.

Bullshit.

The truth is—the first step out of the cage feels like dying.

It's ripping off armor you've worn so long it's fused to your skin.
It's stepping into air so raw it strips your lungs bare.
It's leaving behind everything you built to survive, even the pieces that kept you alive when nothing else could.

And it hurts.
Like hell.

Because the cage—even when you hated it—was familiar.
Painful? Yes.
Limiting? Yes.
But you knew the rules.
You knew how to survive there.

Out here?

No maps. No guarantees. No one telling you who to be or how to act.

Just you.
Raw. Untamed. Alive.

The first step isn't graceful.
It's not brave in the way movies like to show it.

It's clumsy, ugly, a half-fall, half-leap with your heart hammering in your throat and every voice from your past screaming at you to turn back.

And part of you will want to.

Because pain has a memory.
It will remind you of every time you dared before and got burned.
It will whisper that it's safer to go back to the cage you know than gamble everything on a freedom that might just break you.

But here's the thing:
The pain of that first step is nothing compared to the agony of standing still.

Nothing compares to the slow, grinding death of shrinking yourself down, year after year, until there's nothing left but a ghost of who you were supposed to be.

You've already hurt.
You've already bled.
You've already paid the price for someone else's comfort.

Now it's time to hurt for you.
To hurt forward.
To burn for your own damn life.

LIVING OUT LOUD

Because pain with purpose?
That's power.

You will stumble.
You will question yourself.
You will feel alone, some days more than you think you can bear.

But every step you take—even the broken ones, even the shaking ones—tears another piece of that old cage apart.

You aren't dying.
You're *waking up*.

And it's supposed to hurt.
It's supposed to strip you down to your core so you can finally rebuild in your own image—not theirs.

The first step hurts like hell.
Take it anyway.

The fire is waiting.

PART THREE
BECOMING THE FIRE

ELEVEN
LIVING ON FIRE

You don't crawl once you've tasted flight.

You don't tiptoe through life after you've walked through your own fear and come out the other side still burning.

Once you break the chains and take that first step through hell and don't turn back—
you change.

Living unchained isn't about being *reckless*.
It's about being *relentless*.
It's about waking up every damn day with the fire still in your chest and refusing to apologize for it.

No more shrinking.
No more doubting.
No more watering yourself down to make the world comfortable.

You were never meant to fit in a cage.
You were meant to *ignite the air* on fire just by breathing.

Living on fire means speaking your truth, even when your voice shakes.
It means choosing yourself, even when the world calls you selfish.

It means creating a life so alive, so honest, so wild, that small minds can't survive in your presence.

They'll call you too much.
They'll call you unstable, dramatic, dangerous.

Good.

Let them.

Because living on fire is dangerous—
Dangerous to fear.
Dangerous to lies.
Dangerous to anyone who built their comfort on your silence.

The ones who need you to stay small will call you selfish the moment you stop sacrificing yourself for their story.
Let them choke on their own comfort.

You don't owe anyone your fire.

Living on fire isn't clean.
It's messy.
It's imperfect.
It's scars and ashes and rebirth, all wrapped up in a life that feels too big to name.

And that's exactly the point.
You're not supposed to be easy to explain.

You're supposed to burn so brightly that the world either catches fire with you—or gets the hell out of your way.

No waiting.
No permission.
No applause.

LIVING OUT LOUD

Just fire.

You are the spark.
You are the storm.
You are the *revolution you've been waiting for*.

So keep burning.
Keep choosing the flames over the cage.
Keep living so loudly that the ones still trapped in their fear have no choice but to notice—
to feel it.
To remember what fire taste like.

And maybe—just maybe—
they'll start a fire of their own.

TWELVE
THE SILENCE AFTER

When the fire dies down,
there's no applause.
Just quiet.
Stillness that you'll swear is punishment.
Because you've never known peace that didn't feel like absence.

You'll pace.
You'll overthink.
You'll try to rebuild old cages—
because you miss the structure,
even if it bled you dry.

You'll second-guess the silence.
You'll wonder if you made it all up—
if the fire was ever real,
if the pain was ever enough.

Memory will try to rewrite it.
Nostalgia will lie to you.
The loneliness will whisper:
At least you were held there,
even if it was in chains.

Don't fall for it.

That voice is not your friend.
It's your trauma—dressed as longing.

You are not weak for missing what broke you.
But you are not meant to go back.

Let the silence stretch.
Let it ache.
Let it teach you how to be whole
without permission,
without pattern,
without performing for someone else's comfort.

This is the space where you learn to live.
And this time, it's yours.

THIRTEEN
BORN OF FIRE

You weren't broken by the fire,
you were *forged* by it.

Everything they thought would destroy you—
the shame, the silence, the expectations—
didn't weaken you.
It tempered you.

You're not the same person who entered the flames.
You're something harder now.
Something sharper.
Something undeniable.

They don't get to touch you anymore.

Not the ones who doubted you.
Not the ones who tried to shape you.
Not even the ones you loved—who only loved your chains.

You belong to the fire now.
To yourself.
To the truth you fought tooth and nail to claim.

This isn't survival anymore.

This isn't just staying alive.

This is living on your own damn terms.

This is breathing without flinching.
This is speaking without swallowing the words first.
This is occupying every inch of space you were told to apologize for.

This is being.
Without permission.
Without apology.
Without fear.

And let me tell you something:
The world isn't ready for the version of you that walks out of the fire.

Good.

They don't deserve to be ready.

Because you didn't survive all of it just to be palatable.
You didn't fight your way through smoke and ash to fit neatly into their expectations.

You survived to shatter them.
You survived to scare them.
You survived to show them what happens when someone who was never meant to burn *becomes the flame itself.*

No chains.
No apologies.
No shame.

Only fire.

Only truth.

Only you—unforgiven, unstoppable, undeniable.

Born of fire.

Built for more.
And just getting started.

FOURTEEN
THE FIREKEEPER

Anyone can burn for a moment.
Anyone can erupt once, light up the sky, and disappear into smoke.

But keeping the fire?
That's something else entirely.

Because after the rebirth—after you rise from ash and ruin and call yourself whole—you learn that living unchained isn't just about setting fire to what held you back.
It's about tending that fire. Every day. Purposefully.

This is where the myth ends and the truth begins.

The firekeeper doesn't chase flames—they sustain them.

They know the difference between reckless burning and sacred heat.
They know that power without grounding will scorch the very soul it came to save.

So they do the work. Quietly. Repeatedly. And without applause.

Because keeping the fire isn't about being seen.
It's about being centered.

It's holding space for your own fire through the silence, through the storm, through the stillness that comes after the chaos fades.

It's choosing yourself, again and again—
even when no one is watching.
Even when no one understands.
Even when your fire flickers—low and quiet—
and the shadows try to convince you it's gone.

It isn't.

It never was.

It just needed tending.
It needed you—not raging, not screaming, not breaking—but committing.

This is the part no one glamorizes, because it's not sexy to stay.
Consistency is not marketable.[A1]
Nor is showing up for your own healing every day without making it a performance.

But this is where freedom becomes real.
Not in the explosion—but in the devotion.
In the daily return to yourself.

In the rituals you build to protect your fire.
The boundaries you no longer explain.
The choices that honor your growth, even when they cost you company.

This is the chapter where you stop asking the world for permission to exist as you are.

You already burned down the cages.
Now you must build a life that holds your flame without smothering

it.

You become the keeper of your own light.

And you learn—
Not every day will blaze.

Some will be embers.
Some, barely a spark.

But that's okay.

Because you know how to stoke the heat.
Because you know how to stay lit, even when the wind howls.
Because you've stopped depending on the world to feed you.

You've learned to feed yourself.

The firekeeper doesn't chase chaos.
They choose presence.
They choose peace—not the kind that silences the truth, but the kind that sustains it.

This is not the beginning.
This is not the end.
This is what happens when you stop surviving, and start living.
This is what happens when the fire becomes yours.

So, stay lit.

Stay fierce.

Stay the keeper of everything you've fought to become.
And never let them convince you that the quiet power you've built isn't enough.

DRAY ORION

Because it is.
It always was.
And now, you know how to keep it.

Because you became it.

FIFTEEN
THE WAY YOU BURN

There's a difference between burning out and burning through.

This part of the story isn't about proving anything.
It's about owning everything.

Because the way you burn now—
it's not desperate, it's deliberate.
Not for attention.
For alignment.

You've already scorched the lies.
Melted the masks.
What remains is heat with intention—
a blaze that bends, but doesn't break.

You don't owe anyone a performance.
You don't have to collapse to be valid.
You don't have to rise in public just to be seen.

You've learned the strongest fire is the one you tend in silence—
the one no one understands,
but still feels when they get too close.

This is the fire that doesn't ask for forgiveness.

Doesn't dim when it's inconvenient.

It lives in your choices now—
how you love, leave, and speak your name with both hands open
and zero apology.

The way you burn now doesn't demand the world to change first.
It changes you.
And that's enough.

Because this flame isn't about rage anymore.
It's about release.
Letting go of the need to be explained,
accepted,
tamed.

The way you burn now heals what the old fire couldn't touch.
It lives in your boundaries,
in your no's,
in your refusal to shrink.
You've outgrown the kind of fire
that needs to engulf everything to feel alive.

Now—
you create warmth.
Now—
you choose what gets lit.
Now—
you're the match and the spark,
the flame and the fuel.

And anyone who tries to contain you?
They were never strong enough for this version of you anyway.

So, burn like that.
Burn in a way that builds.

Burn in a way that softens and sharpens at once.
Burn in a way only those who've done their own burning
can understand.

The way you burn now is with a truth they'll never silence.

And that?
That's the most dangerous thing of all.

SIXTEEN
LIVING OUT LOUD

Living out loud is the final rebellion.

Not the loud that begs for attention,
the kind that refuses to shrink.

The loud that doesn't wait for approval.
The loud that walks into every room already knowing its worth.

Living out loud means you stop dressing your truth in apologies.
You stop dimming your joy to keep the bitter comfortable.
You stop breaking yourself into pieces just so someone else can feel whole.

This is where everything changes.
This is where you stop surviving for others, and start living for yourself.
Unapologetically. Unconditionally. Unchained.

They told you to be quiet.
To behave.
To soften your edges.
To bury your fire and call it maturity.

They lied.

Because living out loud isn't reckless.
It's righteous.

It's what happens when you remember that your voice wasn't made for silence.
That your skin isn't a cage.
That your spirit isn't something to be negotiated.

You don't live out loud because it's easy.
You live out loud because you've been silent too long.

Because every time you muted your truth to make someone else comfortable, a piece of you went missing.

Living out loud is gathering every broken piece, every buried scream, every no you swallowed when you should've roared—and setting it all free.

It's being your full damn self, even when the world calls it too much.

Too loud.
Too weird.
Too real.

Good.

Let it be too much.
Let it scare them.

Because you weren't built to be understood by a world that survives on silence.
You were built to shake it.
To unsettle it.
To light it up and walk through it, unafraid.

LIVING OUT LOUD

Living out loud is the moment you realize:
You are the miracle.
You are the masterpiece.

You are both storm and shelter.[A1]

You don't need to be tamed.
You need to be seen.
Heard.

Held in your wholeness—first and always, by you.

So here's your permission slip, in case you still think you need one:

Live.
Live as if they're watching.
Live as if they're not.

Live like the fire in your chest is holy—*because it is.*
Live like your joy is sacred—*because it is.*
Live like your scars tell stories worth hearing—*because they do.*

Don't just exist.
Don't just go through the motions.
Don't just survive in rooms where your silence is more valued than your voice.

Set the tone.
Shake the floor.
Burn bright, burn true, burn loud.

Live out loud.
Because anything less?
Was never living at all

EPILOGUE
A LETTER TO THE ONE STILL BURNING

Hey you,

If you made it here, I need you to know something:

You are not broken.
You are not too much.
You are not lost beyond repair.

You are becoming.

These pages were written with blood and bone—with the fire I once thought would kill me, and the truth I had to fight like hell to claim. I didn't write this for applause. I wrote this so you'd never again feel like the only one dragging your chains through the dark, wondering if freedom was just a pretty lie.

It's not.

Freedom is real—but it costs.
It costs certainty.

It costs comfort.
It costs the version of you they taught you to perform instead of be.

But if you're still here, I know you're willing to pay it.
I know you're ready. Maybe not all at once. And maybe not loudly.
But still—you're ready.

Ready to stop asking for permission.
Ready to stop shrinking.
Ready to burn for the life that was always yours.

Let them call you selfish.
Let them say you've changed.
You're not here to be understood.
You're here to live out loud.

To be seen, not sanitized.
To be free, not filtered.

Don't go back to the cage just because it's quiet there.
Don't trade your fire for anyone's comfort.

You owe them nothing.
You owe yourself everything.

If this world doesn't have room for the real you, then set it on fire and build your own.

And when the silence creeps in—because it will—remember this:
You're not alone.

I walked through it, too.
I bled for this, too.
I burned for this, too.

So light your fire.

Tend it fiercely.
And never let anyone convince you to dim.

Because now you know:
There is no shame.
There are no chains.
There is only the truth—
and the roar of your own voice,
finally blazing through.

See you in the blaze,

~ DRAY ORION

Made in United States
Orlando, FL
03 July 2025